CROSSOVER TO SUCCESS

Charleston, SC
www.PalmettoPublishing.com

Crossover to Success
Copyright © 2023 by Jimmie L. Lucas

All rights reserved

No portion of this book may be reproduced, stored in a retrieval system, or transmitted in any form by any means–electronic, mechanical, photocopy, recording, or other–except for brief quotations in printed reviews, without prior permission of the author.

Paperback ISBN: 979-8-8229-1089-8
eBook ISBN: 979-8-8229-1099-7

CROSSOVER TO SUCCESS

The 7 Things You Need To Know Before You Step On The Basketball Court

JIMMIE L. LUCAS

TABLE OF CONTENTS

PRE-GAME WARM-UPS	1
INTRODUCTION	3
FIRST QUARTER	7
CHAPTER 1: Capability	9
CHAPTER 2: Confidence	13
SECOND QUARTER	19
CHAPTER 3: Consistency	21
HALF-TIME	25
THIRD QUARTER	27
CHAPTER 4: Commitment	29
CHAPTER 5: Character	33
FOURTH QUARTER	39
CHAPTER 6: Cost	41
CHAPTER 7: Communication	45
OVERTIME	51
CLOSING	53
POST GAME COOL DOWN	57
ACKNOWLEDGEMENT	59
FINAL THOUGHTS	61
ABOUT THE AUTHOR	63

PRE-GAME WARM-UPS

"THE BLUEPRINT FOR SUCCESS STARTS WITH DREAMS, HARD WORK, FUNDAMENTALS, AND DISCIPLINE. IT'S FOUNDATION STANDS ON RESPECT, GOALS, TENACITY, WILL, AND DETERMINATION. FOREVER STANDS TALL BY LEADERSHIP. SELFLESSNESS, SACRIFICE, AND TEAM WORK!!!"

Jimmie L. Lucas

INTRODUCTION

"SUCCESS COMES FROM KNOWING
THAT YOU DID YOUR BEST
TO BECOME THE BEST THAT
YOU ARE CAPABLE OF BECOMING"

John Wooden

Becoming a successful basketball player details a lot of things. Although you must be able to handle the ball, shoot high percentage shots, and play great defense, the one most important factor you must have are the abilities to process the game quickly and react instinctively to every situation regardless of the clock and the score. Learning and understanding **CAPABILITY, CONFIDENCE, CONSISTENCY, COMMITMENT, CHARACTER, COST,** and **COMMUNICATION**, will lead to top performance on and off the basketball court.

As you grow through your basketball career, learn, and put to practice the 7 Cs of Success. You may encounter many defeats and down falls. Michael Jordan once said something about how, "It was not the successes that made him great, but rather it was the defeats and the experience and knowledge he learned from each defeat." Even in defeat you must stay mentally tough, emotionally positive and continue to trust the process.

Staying positive refers to a mindset or attitude that is always looking for the best in every situation, even though that situation may seem negative. Also, staying positive means that your attitude about those negative situations will prevail no matter what the situation is encountered on the court, in the classroom, in the community, or amongst peers.

Before I go into the 7 Cs of Success, you must first understand what staying positive is about. Staying positive about yourself and keeping a certain level of confidence (**not conceitedness**) will go along way in truly understanding and living to the full realm of the 7 Cs of Success. Staying positive is absolutely critical to both achieving and sustaining success in any area of your life. There are two main areas of what it takes to stay truly positive in obtaining your goals that we will explore.

1. It takes a tremendous amount of self-discipline and energy to stay positive.

    Your daily life will be filled with parents wanting you to follow in their footsteps and be a doctor, professional athlete, or military veteran. In some cases, they will overburden you with information that will be an attempt to steer you away from the direction they went in. You teachers and coaches will constantly be on you to, "do what it takes" to be "all you can be". Finally, your peer groups and so called "friends" will be on you to hang out late, skip class, and try drugs and alcohol in order to fit in and be "down" with them.

    Your level of self-discipline will determine which road you choose to go down. Parents, teachers, and coaches are not attempting to run or control your life, but rather allow you to have choices and options on how to send your life in a direction of being successful. If anyone within your peer group is involved in getting bad grades, skipping school, hanging out late, wearing pants off their butts, experimenting with drugs and alcohol, this should no longer be you peer group. Self-discipline involves going against the most popular and surrounding yourself with peers that have the same positive dreams and goals that you have, ones that truly understand and live the 7 Cs of Success.

2. Make up your mind that you are going to do it and stick to it.

    The easiest thing for someone to do is say that they have goals and dreams. Everyone in the world has a dream or a goal that they have once set for themselves. However, the problem is not setting up goals and having dreams, the problem easily becomes being disciplined enough to stick to those dreams and goals. You may start your day with positive thoughts in your mind and a plan to follow. What happens is once you enter into the world, the people you encounter may not share those same dreams and goals as you have. Instead, they want you to follow them and go down their path.

That is where self-discipline and the 7 Cs of Success come into play. Being able to be disciplined enough to do the non-popular thing and positive enough about who you are and the person you want to become allows you to go down a different path then everyone else.

The important distinction to make here is that the discipline it takes in being positive is completely different then the self-discipline it takes to stay positive.

Any basketball player can be positive and confident but only the special ones can stay positive when things get tough, like when your shot is not falling or if your coach has put you on the bench because of your many mistakes. It becomes very easy to become frustrated, make excuses, give up, and become negative. However, the 7 Cs of Success shows you how to avoid this, how to not only constantly always stay positive through any situation, but also how to make positivity contagious amongst your peers and teammates, and not allow negativity to drag you down.

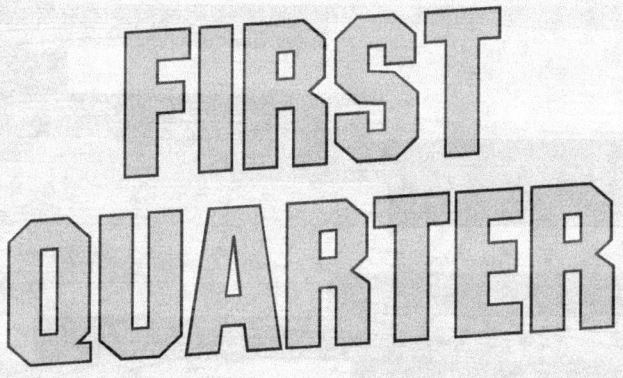

FIRST QUARTER

"IF ALL YOU ARE REMEMBERED FOR IS BEING A GOOD BASKETBALL PLAYER, THEN YOU HAVE DONE A BAD JOB WITH THE REST OF YOUR LIFE"

Isiah Thomas

CHAPTER 1
CAPABILITY

> "ONE SHOULD STRIVE TO IMPROVE ONE'S CAPABILITIES. ONE SHOULD ENHANCE HIS ABILITIES ONLY IN THE POSITIVE DIRECTION."
>
> Rig Veda

As I entered my senior year in high school, I was a three-year Letterman in track and soccer. My ability in doing these sports were very high and I was vey good at them. Coaches said that I had the capability of doing both at the next level.

The problem is that I never lived up to that capability because at the time, football and basketball were the most popular sports. My entire peer group all played these sports and ridiculed me for not playing them over the past three years.

Although I had great self-discipline and confidence on the field of play, within my peer group I lacked that same confidence and discipline to do the non-popular thing.

Giving in to the pressure from my peers, I decided to take my abilities to the basketball court just to show them how capable I was in doing their sport. As a result, not only did I miss out on my fourth consecutive letter and all-state team in soccer, but I also rode the bench on the basketball team for my entire senior season.

We all have the capability to do something or not do something. I can imagine that it has been numerous of times when you were asked to do something on the court or in the classroom and you felt like you just were not capable of doing it. Because of this lack of self-confidence, no matter how hard you worked, you still performed below the coaches' and teachers' expectations.

When this happens, stay within your abilities, and do not become frustrated. Never quit or give up, because only you have the capabilities within yourself to refocus and set attainable goals. Never underestimate you potential and ability, and most importantly, never allow anyone else to underestimate you either. Instead, remember to stay positive and continue to put the time and work in. We are all capable of giving better efforts. We all have the capability to run one more suicide, shoot one hundred more shots, study for thirty more minutes, and give a lot more in practice. Continue to have that basic understanding that you cannot move from your current ability to full potential ability in a day or even a month. It takes maximum self-discipline and time, and you have the capability to understand this and trust the process.

My point is that although you may have the capability to knock down an open jumper, play lock down defense, or lead your team in scoring, without self-confidence this leads to sitting at the end of the bench. Your self-confidence will force you to stick with the unpopular thing and in turn prove to your peer group that doing what is the most popular is not always doing what is right for you.

Having capability gives you no limits as to what you can achieve or accomplish. It has no limitations or boundaries. It is merely being capable to excel in any and everything you work hard enough to obtain.

For example, if you are 5-foot-7 inches, you still posses the capability within yourself to win a slam-dunk contest. Or, if you are a 7-foot-3, you can win a three-point shoot out.

Capabilities do not recognize if you are tall, short, fast, or slow, it only knows preparation, hard work, execution and never giving in to the limitations people may place on your abilities. However, capabilities can and will be copied and imitated, regardless of if it is positive or negative. If you are a good teammate and leader, your teammates will be given the capability to emulate you. As a result, they too will become good teammates and players. In contrary, if you are a bad teammate and poor leader, your teammates will show capabilities of being bad teammates and poor players.

Unlike the mental approach it takes to stay positive, capabilities are simple and, in most cases, very recognizable. You use many of your capabilities all the time. However, to be successful you cannot manufacture or hope that your capability will automatically make you successful. For being capable of shooting high percentage shots, is not the same as being able to shoot high percentage shots. All basketball players are capable, but dedication, hard work, preparation, and discipline makes you able.

CHAPTER 2

CONFIDENCE

> "ONE IMPORTANT KEY TO SUCCESS IS SELF-CONFIDENCE. AN IMPORTANT KEY TO SELF-CONFIDENCE IS PREPARATION."
>
> Arthur Ashe

As you watch and emulate your favorite National Basketball Association (NBA) player, one thing you may notice is an extreme level of confidence. LeBron James and Kevin Durant, to name a couple, are probably two of the most confident players there are. Yes, others in the NBA have confidence in themselves and their abilities or they would not be in the NBA. However, "King James" and "KD", seem to many as being too confident and therefore are considered conceited. Their walk and swagger on the court and their tone and demeanor during interviews have given some followers the perception of arrogance and over-confidence. As those of us that are true NBA fans know, they are far from being conceited and merely possess the top level of confidence in their abilities that it takes to be considered one of the greatest. They have the belief that they are very capable of doing whatever they choose on the basketball court and in life. They have that self-confidence within themselves that they have the ability to perform on and off the court in a very successful way.

As a basketball player, scholar, or anything you so choose in life, having super self-confidence is essential and indispensable for successful performance. You must believe in yourself first, your abilities second, and not allow that belief be blocked by anyone or any situation.

Sometimes you will have those moments where things are not going right. You may begin to lose faith due to bad play or negative comments from opponents, teammates, coaches, and parents. Embarrassing moments can chew at your psyche and destroy the self-confidence which is needed for success during competition. When these moments occur, your ability to have great self-confidence is what will get you through tough times. Continue to work out, continue to shoot extra shots, continue to believe in your capabilities and as a result, you will be a better player, person, and teammate than you could ever imagine.

What you must take from this chapter is what having confidence in your abilities really means. Confidence is not saying you are the best, saying no one can stop you, saying you own the court. Those things are good to believe, but once faced with adversity; those things may hurt you more then help.

True self-confidence is truly believing that the next shot will go in after you miss five in a row; that after four turnovers, your next pass will lead to a dunk; or that you will hit free throws in the final minutes. Having the confidence that the coaching staff, fans, and your teammates believe in you that in the last three minutes, you will make the right plays to secure a win.

You must understand from this that confidence is mostly based on nothing other then a perception, and a belief that you must have in yourself. You may go and download the exact shooting workout done by Steph Curry, but if you do not believe that you have the ability to perform at the same level as Curry, then the workouts are useless. You may have friends who play on other teams that are on long winning streaks, yet they tell you constantly that they feel like they are not fitting in or that the coach does not like them. Although the team is feeling great confidence while having success, your friend lacks self-confidence. Now on the other hand, your team may be on a tremendous losing streak, yet you are in the gym before and after practice putting in the extra work, while having the belief that you will lead your team to the next victory.

My point is that the situation does not depict the confidence level needed for top performance. Only you can control how high or low your self-confidence and self-worth is to your team and society. Self-confidence should not be more or less depending on the situation. In fact, self-confidence should be high or low depending on the individual's abilities. The confidence you have in your abilities in the closing moments and not the opening is what counts. Your perception of yourself is what drives the mind to believe that your current ability level is sufficient to achieve success no matter what the situation may be.

A former coach of mine, when I was playing for an All-Air Force team in Okinawa, Japan, use to say something like "Luck is when opportunity meets preparation". If you truly understand what it means to have self-confidence, then this will apply to you in knowing that when the game is on the line you have prepared up to that point as much as you can, that you have put in the work, and at that moment you do not want to allow the perception of your confidence level stop you from attempting anything. When the coach puts the ball in your hands, when your teammates look at you to save them, your self-confidence does not know luck. It knows repetition, it knows hard work, it knows preparation, and it knows getting the rebound, sinking the free throw or burying the fifteen-footer at the buzzer.

The most important thing to remember is not to be arrogant, believing you are above your teammates and coaches and that you are bigger than the game and the team goals. Also, do not be overconfident, in that you have overbearing confidence in thinking you are above losing and therefore a loss must be the fault of your teammates or coaching strategies. Understand that confidence is self-fulfilling and the higher you put yourself above others the farther you will fall. Do not ever look down upon a teammate or sibling for not having the same confidence as you, because those without it may fail or not try, and you have the capability to help, show, teach, and instill in those close to you your self-confidence and ways for them to obtain it within themselves. When this is done, you as a basketball player, or your sibling, or friend will truly be a champion. Every day, every second, you must take the necessary steps to continue to be a confident player, student, and most importantly, person.

In closing, I leave you with this: Do not get discouraged when your self-confidence is lacking. I sometimes have this doubt as well. However, remember it is the perception of how people see your doubt that will bring that lack of confidence to the light. I will never let someone know that I am having doubt in my abilities. Instead, I step back, remove myself from the moment, then rely on the preparation, the weightlifting at 5:00 a.m., the 200 extra shots at 11:00 p.m. When practice is over, the extra sprints, that extra suicide, the hundred made free throws. The time I get a salad at that popular fast-food restaurant instead of a huge burger or choosing to drink water rather than a soda. At that moment, I begin to believe again in my capabilities. I believe again that I am the hardest working person on the floor, that up until that moment, I have put in the necessary time and preparation to have earned success and my self-confidence is present again. Then I re-enter the moment and go get the ball.

SECOND QUARTER

"A MAN MAKES MISTAKES, BUT HE IS NOT A FAILURE UNTIL HE STARTS BLAMING SOMEONE ELSE."

John Wooden

CHAPTER 3

CONSISTENCY

"IF YOU DON'T HAVE TIME TO DO IT RIGHT, WHEN WILL YOU EVER HAVE TIME TO DO IT OVER?"

John Wooden

The hardest thing to be the most consistent with in basketball is a triple double. Being able to have double-digit numbers in points, rebounds, assist, or steals is a very difficult thing to do. Most players like Michael Jordan can consistently lead the league in scoring over a season, or Jason Kidd can consistently lead the league in assist over an entire season. Even Dwight Howard has led the league in rebounding for the whole season. But during the 2016-17 NBA season, Russell Westbrook became one of two players, the other being Oscar Robertson, to averaged a triple double for the entire season. This means that he consistently scored more then ten points, grabbed more then ten rebounds, as well as passed the ball more then ten times that led to scores every game of the season. The consistency it takes to do this is bigger than any other single feet in the NBA past or present, and that is including Wilt Chamberlain scoring 100 points in one game.

In order for you to be able to do the same fete as an NBA player in the future you must be consistent enough to do the right things the right way all the time. There are no taking nights off, skipping practices, or not studying. With many other issues that engulf your daily life, being a consistent player becomes a very hard thing to do. See, becoming a great basketball player, is bigger than the consistent numbers you put up on the court. Becoming a great player typically starts with how consistent you are off the court. Are you keeping your grades up to remain academically eligible? Are you obeying your parents and consistently giving them or rather showing them how grateful you are to them for dropping you off and picking you up for practice, spending extra money on shoes and backpacks? Are you getting proper rest instead of up all night playing video games? Are your eating habits aiding to your bodies development or hurting it?

In addition, you must have the self-discipline to work on your game everyday, regardless of what friends and family might say. Even if you do not have access to a gym daily, is not an excuse for not getting better. You can consistently work at home on ball handling drills, getting stronger and watching game films. You must be willing to make consistent sacrifices in order to achieve your ultimate goals. That sacrifice comes in the form of consistently working until all dreams and goals are accomplished and all boundaries have been knocked down.

The most important thing to remember is that consistency does not just apply to one aspect of your game and life. Just working on your jump shot on a consistent basis is not what having consistency is completely about. Working on just part of your game is still a good thing; however, it does not get you to averaging a triple-double for an entire season. You must consistently eat correctly, rest plenty, make good grades, and stay away from peer pressure, and constantly workout and practice in order to re-live a historic 2016-17 season.

As we look at consistency a little deeper, we will find that consistency does not apply to just physical and external conditions. There is also the need for inner consistency and the need for values, attitudes, and beliefs to be in line with each other. The inner things that are hidden from public view must also remain consistent with your goals. You must believe that shooting every day will make you a great shooter and not just because your coach or I are telling you it will. Your attitude and values must be ones that consistently gets you going to the gym, puts your nose in the book, and says no to drugs and alcohol.

Without your inner values and beliefs, being on the same page with your daily actions, you are preparing to fail and not excel. You are going to be faced with many difficult problems that you may feel are unexplainable. If you think highly of yourself as a player but perform badly on the court, then your inner and external beliefs have no consistency and lacks confidence. As a result, that high thinking will turn into self doubt. It is not good enough for you to just believe in your abilities, you must also believe in yourself.

Consistency is the most complex and the most difficult to completely understand and do on a regular basis for basketball players. The reason for this is because you can still be a very good player without fully understanding consistency or even consistently doing it completely. You can have a good jump shot simply by working on your shot daily even though you stay up all night playing video games and eating junk food. You might even be a very good high school player because of your gifted skills even though you may not believe that you are. In some cases, players such as this go on to play in college and might even be NBA players. The difference is whether or not you are satisfied with being an NBA player or are your dreams and goals more consistent with not being the next Russell Westbrook to average a triple-double for an entire season but rather be the first to average a triple-double for an entire career.

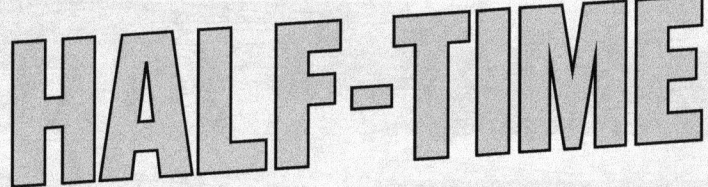

"PEOPLE OFTEN SAY THAT THIS PERSON OR THAT PERSON HAS NOT YET FOUND HIMSELF. BUT THE SELF IS NOT SOMETHING THAT ONE FINDS. IT IS SOMETHING THAT ONE CREATES."

Thomas Szasz

"I CAN ACCEPT FAILURE,
EVERYONE FAILS AT SOMETHING,
BUT I CAN'T ACCEPT NOT TRYING."

- Michael Jordan

CHAPTER 4

COMMITMENT

> "THE KEY IS NOT THE "WILL TO WIN"- EVERYBODY HAS THAT, THE KEY IS THE WILL TO PREPARE TO WIN THAT IS IMPORTANT."
>
> Bobby Knight

The late great, and amazing Kobe Bryant's commitment to the NBA came long before he decided to not go to college and instead enter the NBA straight out of high school in 1996. Being the son of a former NBA player, Kobe committed to being the world's greatest player started unknowingly at age three, while his dad Joe "Jellybean" Bryant was playing for the Philadelphia 76ers. The commitment to excellence continued when at age seven his family moved to Italy, and he continued to improve his basketball abilities on a global stage. Even to date of the book being published, years after his untimely and tragic death, Kobe "The Black Mamba" Bryant is regarded as one of the greatest best basketball players to have ever done. Probably even, the closest there is to a Jordan comparison. The journey did not come without a tremendous amount of sacrifice and a top level of commitment to not just be an NBA player, but rather be known as one of the greatest of all time.

When you make a commitment to be great at something, it does not happen by sitting around and wishing it would come true. If you make a commitment to get all A's, then you must commit to dedicating the majority of your time to studying. Likewise, if you get all F's, then you have simply made that commitment of not studying at all. It does not matter if it is athletics or academics, entertainment, or athletics, you must fully commit to it. Once you commit, you are bonded by your word, heart, and soul. You should be making a pledge and commitment to be fully involved and tuned in to that burning desire. You must stay the course, while putting every bit of energy within you into being successful, just as Kobe Bryant did every day once he made the commitment to skip college and enter the NBA draft.

Although Kobe's Los Angeles Lakers team would have great success during his career in the league, continued and consistent success was not always the result. However, his commitment to getting back to the NBA Finals, and relentless work ethic of going out and doing it again and again eventually paid off. I am sure he would tell you that the payoff has been worth the sacrifice and self-discipline.

Basketball is not the only part of your life you can commit to. Along with basketball, you must be willing and flexible enough to commit to making good grades, committed to listening and obeying your parents, committed to being a model citizen, and committed fully to achieving your dreams and goals. You must be committed to the point that you will have enough self-discipline to continue to become a better person and player every single day. Those that truly are committed will not allow any distractions from the outside world block their will, determination, and self-confidence.

Although this thought process became true for Kobe's overall success on the basketball court, without the proper level of sacrifices, discipline, and confidence, for you it will be even more difficult to obtain. Out of all the 7 Cs, commitment is one of the top words you must fully understand to achieve great success. Without commitment, there is no action and without action there is no success. Being fully committed on the basketball court as a team leader is the action that sets all other things in motion. After that pledge of leadership is made, a specific way of conduct is to follow. First, your beliefs and values must again be in line with your actions. Not only do you have to show it, but you also have to fully believe in your abilities, and the abilities of your teammates. All-time greats like Larry Bird, Magic Johnson, Michael Jordan, and even LeBron James have the uncanny ability to make those around them better players. Their commitment to excellence internally aligns with their actions externally. If a teammate sees them diving for loose balls, then they feel like they must do the same thing. Likewise, if fully committed players and leaders are always early for practice and stay late to shoot extra shots, then when the coach blows the whistle to go home, other players will also decide to stay for extra shooting.

The two most important things to remember when it comes to being a committed and effective leader are:

1. Your values, beliefs, and principles must be concrete and unbreakable on and off the court. There must be a top level of self-discipline, self-confidence, and sacrifice. These things cannot be changed or broken by any negative person or set back.

2. Deep within yourself you must be committed to obtaining all goals and dreams. Allow your actions to be true to who you are as a person. Never take the form of someone else or adhere to a set of beliefs that are not your own.

This can get confusing in that on some teams you may not be the leader but find yourself just another piece to the puzzle. This does not mean going against the team goals for your own personal gains, but instead, being a positive influence on the team as well as a great teammate. Combine your commitments of excellence, sacrifice and dedication with that of the team's, and make it one. Remember, all things are difficult before they are easy, and therefore if you are committed to winning but find yourself on a team that loses a lot of games do not quit or blame your teammates; it simply means that you need to share your commitment to winning with the rest of your team. The most effective leaders have a strong sense of integrity and self-confidence. You won't allow losing to become acceptable without personally trying to do everything you can to change the atmosphere by changing the attitudes. By doing this, it will lead to a willingness to spread the credit of success to your teammates. As one success turns into two, more people will start to buy into it. In the end, this will lead to championships.

Although you may be fully committed internally, this is most difficult to show during times when there are high numbers of losses. However, when that losing turns into winning, it is the most readily proven. If you can keep your head held high and the emotions of your teammates positive, it will demonstrate how strong your belief of commitment is during tough times. The tough times are the ones where true leaders stand out and be known. True commitment is not simply saying "I will be a leader and lead my team to victory." True commitment, true leadership, is showing your team the right way through sacrifice, self-discipline, and most importantly as a team.

CHAPTER 5

CHARACTER

"WATCH YOUR THOUGHTS, FOR THEY BECOME YOUR WORDS. WATCH YOUR WORDS, FOR THEY BECOME YOUR ACTIONS. WATCH YOUR ACTIONS, FOR THEY BECOME YOUR HABITS. WATCH YOUR HABITS, FOR THEY BECOME YOUR CHARACTER. WATCH YOUR CHARACTER, FOR IT BECOMES YOUR DESTINY."

Unknown

In my opinion, the most important factor on having longevity in being successful is how your character stacks up against your actions. Coach John Wooden, who is a Hall of Fame college basketball coach, having won ten National Championships at UCLA in twelve years, once said, "Be more concerned with your character than your reputation, because your character is what you really are while your reputation is merely what others think you are."

Coach Wooden really understood what being successful was all about. He knew and tried to get his players to understand that the things you did off the court weighed more heavily than those done on the court. Also, he understood the fact that your character will depict your reactions during times of hardship. A person with good character will persevere and have the will to keep going during those times when all seems lost. They will search for answers and not excuses. They will trust the process.

To fully understand what character really is and how it applies to your play on the court and your quality of life off the court, there are four things I believe that you must know that come directly along with what being a person of character is all about. If you are a true person of character these things will be easy for you to do on a daily basis. Once they are done on a consistent basis, not only will you more often than not be a winner on the basketball court as a leader, but also a winner in the unpredictable game of life.

The first important factor under character is being **trustworthy**. When you are trustworthy, you fulfill and complete all obligations you commit to. If you say you are going to help a friend study geometry, you do not make an excuse when the time comes to meet. If your coach asks you to mentor a freshman, you do not take him to a party and leave him for hours while you run off with your girlfriend. Being trustworthy is often the most difficult thing to do because it takes a great deal of honesty and integrity.

Respect is the next thing that falls under what being a person of character is all about. The thing about respect is that we all think that people should automatically give us respect. The problem with this is that respect is not given; it is by all accounts earned. True respect comes from your commitment, along with your consistent pursuit to be the best at what you decide to be. You just do not get respect because you can play basketball at a high level, or you make all A's in school. It comes from not what you do to help yourself be the best, but more from what you do to help others become the best they can become.

Your parents may always throw the word "**responsibility**" around quite often. Most times it probably just enters in one ear and never registers. Well, by taking the step in reading this book you have unknowingly taken the responsibility upon yourself to become a better leader on and off the basketball court **(WAIT! DO NOT PUT THE BOOK DOWN! KEEP READING!)**. When you take on responsibility, you take on things that are both good and bad. You are placed with what may seem like a tremendous amount of weight on your shoulders of peoples' tasks, problems, and expectations. It may feel like it is too much to handle at such a young age. The thing about being a person of character is when you are taking on responsibilities of not just your own but also of others, at times it comes easy and is welcomed. The reason for this is because you do not look at it as a negative, overwhelming thing, but instead as a way to continue to grow into a person whose long-term goals are those of being successful on and off the court. You understand and realize that your commitment to excellence, consistent pursuit of greatness, unbreakable confidence, capability to overcome, and a character unlike no other will and does give you the right as well as put you in a position to stay the course. In the end parents, coaches, teachers, and teammates will also give you the respect you have earned in helping others and making those around you become better players, and more importantly, better people.

Although you would really like for your life to just be the basketball court and your bedroom, unfortunately it is not. You have a daily commitment to be out in public amongst peers, adults from your school, coaches and teammates, and strangers at stores and various places within the community. A person of character should always be a **good citizen**. As part of a community, you have a responsibility to be a model citizen. Along with that means that you hold your friends to the same standards of conduct you uphold, too, when they think that no one is looking. Get out and do some volunteer work with the youth, homeless, veterans, or the elderly. See if any help is needed with setting up for other school activities that involve non-basketball sports as well as different clubs such as drama and music clubs, or the debate team. Show that you are a true leader by even getting your teammates involved along with you. Whatever the case may be, do not stop by being a positive influence on the basketball court, but instead get out within the different areas of the community and make a positive difference in other people lives for no other reason other then because it is simply, "the right thing to do."

By now, you may be thinking that you did not sign up for this and that you just wanted to be a basketball player. This is to be expected. However, this is also the reason you decided to read my book. If your intent is to be just a basketball player, then do not waste another minute reading. Forget everything you have learned up until now and go outside to the local court with the rest of your friends and continue to pick up bad habits by playing street ball. You will have a nice high school career that will come to an end as soon as the coach makes you turn your uniform in.

On the other hand, if your intent is to play in college, and have longevity in the NBA and beyond, you may now be starting to understand the type of hard work, dedication, and sacrifice needed to be successful in this sport I love. Kobe and LeBron did not just wake up one morning and suddenly at the age of 18 say, "You know, I am going to enter the NBA draft and not go to college." No, it was a process they went through, steps they took from the beginning that got them to that point. Believe it or not, it all started with having good character: by being a person of their word and holding themselves accountable to doing the right things, the right way, **ALL** the time. They had the responsibility to do whatever it took to become mentally and physically ready when their names were called. If this is what you truly want and are willing to go out and do all the things necessary, then you can still go to the court with your friends and teach them what you have learned and take them on the journey with you. It will be worth the ride.

FOURTH QUARTER

"YOU HAVE POWERS YOU NEVER DREAMED OF. YOU CAN DO THINGS YOU NEVER THOUGHT YOU COULD DO. THERE ARE NO LIMITATIONS IN WHAT YOU CAN DO EXCEPT THE LIMITATIONS OF YOUR OWN MIND."

Darwin P. Kingsley

CHAPTER 6

COST

> "THE PRICE OF EXCELLENCE IS DISCIPLINE. THE COST OF MEDIOCRITY IS DISAPPOINTMENT."
>
> — William A. Ward

My decision to not play soccer my senior year of high school cost me to miss out on a chance to play major college soccer at a big-time school, or even in the World Cup. Therefore, the cost for not being a man of character, not staying fully committed, and not having the confidence and self-discipline within myself to not listen to my peers and continue to play soccer cost me more at the time then I would have liked.

In the end, you pay for everything you do. Every action or reaction comes with a cost. All the actions you take that are negative come with a consequence. If you make the choice to not study, you get bad grades. If you decide to constantly show up late for practice and give excuse after excuse, you find yourself off the team. If you choose not to work on your game in the summer months, you get cut in the winter months. Even at home your parents make you pay penalties for bad behavior and lack of focus. Every poor performance, regardless of the situation, comes with a high cost of shame and disappointment.

At this point in your life, you may have the mind frame that you are invincible, as if nobody can tell you anything. You believe you have all the answers. Ironically, you are not correct. You absolutely have all the wrong answers because you have not learned enough up until now to know what the right questions are to go with those answers. The cost you will pay in the long run is not worth not knowing what the right questions are. If you surround yourself with positive peers and adults, it will cost you nothing. However, the payoff in the end will be achieving all your goals and dreams.

On the other hand, you may also pay a cost for good behavior. The hard work you put into your training and practices will cost you great pain and fatigue. Time spent away from family and friends may even cost you quality time with them. If you are committed to what the results will be, there will be great compensation for your sacrifices that surpass the other costs. This compensation can be in the form of wins, notoriety, and excellence. It could also be the platform needed to achieve the goals you have set for yourself. Regardless of what you have set your goals to be, reaching these goals comes with a cost. You must remember that you can achieve anything you want when you are willing to pay full price for it. There is no reduced price; there is no discount, only top-of-the-line quality with a top-of-the-line price. Stay committed to your dreams; do not be like me in high school and attempt to live someone else's dream. All successes come with a high price. Nothing comes easy or is free. The more you pay into it, the better the return on investment. So, if you truly want complete success, go for it no matter what the cost. Go all out and pay full price, cut no corners, or look for any shortcuts. Remember the words Coach Wooden uttered long ago when he said that "You only get out of it, what you put into it."

CHAPTER 7

COMMUNICATION

"THE WAY WE COMMUNICATE WITH OTHERS, ULTIMATELY DETERMINES THE QUALITY OF OUR LIVES."

Anthony Robins

The world we live in today has far surpassed picking up a telephone and dialing a number to communicate with others. We are now in the time and age where instant messaging, emails, and texting control our daily lives. However, the one thing that has remained constant in all this is that we must communicate all the time for our lives to be influenced. Whether it is bad or good communication, it remains the number one thing to do other then eating and sleeping. You must communicate with your parents about your needs and wants; your teachers and coaches for growth and direction, your friends about emotions, and even Mr. Joe at the shopping center to have exchange occur. Without the right type of communication, you will not be able to achieve those dreams and goals you are striving for.

I saved communication for last because in my opinion, communication is the number one thing to master when it comes to success. All things that are great in life will come through proper communication. Yes, you can get your mind and body in top shape and ready for maximal performance all by yourself, but you will and must know how to community with everyone to get where you ultimately want to be in life. In the NBA, there is an interview process. The owner and coach will sit down with you to see what type of character you have before they decide to pick you number one. Even before you get that far, college coaches and recruiters will come to your house to meet you to see if your abilities on the court transfer to your character off the court. They do not want players who can not communicate properly because you must be in front of teammates, the media, and fans and if you can not communicate correctly, they will not take you, regardless of your special talents.

What you must remember is that communication is not just being able to put together a proper sentence. Communication is how you dress, your walk, your grooming, and yes, your character. All these things and more fall under proper communication. Please understand that you are not going to be asked to change who you are. Never do that because who you are is what will get you to being recruited in the first place. However, what you will be asked to do is be flexible and adaptive. You need to have the ability to be able to talk Wall Street while on the golf course with a CEO or owner. You must show that you can talk politics with coaches, fans, and boosters, but also be able to ask the cleaning crew and cooks how their day is going. As you come across all types of people from all types of places, you need to have the ability to talk to anyone about anything. That means you must stay on top of current events, the history of your sport, and everything you can find out about team, company, or organization you are going to be apart of. The key, however, is not to talk about things that you do not know. If there is a subject area you are unsure about, never fabricate or make up your own opinion based on nothing but hearsay. Be humble enough to say that you are not sure about that and even ask for an explanation. This will make you look even more approachable than artificial.

Also, when it comes to communication, you need to open and speak up about situations that are important to you, whether it is playing time, a grade you feel that you did not earn, a home issue that is bothering you, or a teammate who will not pass you the ball. To learn answers, you must be a good listener in conjunction with a communicator. By doing this you might just learn something useful, and all the above issues will become better. Always remember to ask and answer questions in a serious manner. By doing this, you will let the person you are communicating with know their opinions are worthwhile and taken into consideration. It may even add to their self-esteem and self-confidence.

On the other hand, be prepared for answers you may not like. Again, remember that we are all different and your view of something will be completely different from other people's view of the same thing. That is what is meant by being a good listener. Express your thoughts and feelings completely, and then allow the other person to express theirs completely before you interrupt. Never be defiant, snobbish, or dismissive. Even if you do not agree, just listen, try, and take from it whatever you can and move on. The key is being able to adjust and adapt in any situation. For example, in your entire youth career, your school coach told you to do a pick-n-roll one way, but when you get to

AAU your coach says do it another way. Well, that AAU coach is not saying you have been doing it the wrong way for all that time. No, that is not what they are saying at all. All they are trying to communicate is that they want you to do it their way, the way that works better for their team. Adjust and adapt and do it the way they want and when you get back to your school team revert to the way your coach for that team wants you to do. They part to this is now you have learned two ways to do one play so once you get to college you become an even more versatile player.

If at any time, there is something that you do not understand; speak up! Whether it is a drill at practice, an out of bounds play under the basket, or even the defensive rotations, ask questions. Do not just sit there like you got it and when it is your turn to perform you mess it all up. As a long-time coach, that is the one thing that gets under my skin the most. When I take time from practice to explain a drill or play, and then I always ask the question, "Does everyone understand? Should I go over it again?" Every time, there are one or two players who get up there and do it completely wrong. Then I must waste more time stopping and explaining it all over again. That gets under my skin, much more then players missing wide open lay-ups. So, if you do not understand, speak up. It will not make you look weak or dumb. I like it when players say they do not understand and to go over it again. That shows me that they are interested in paying attention to detail as well as insuring they handle their part correctly so another player will not have to pick up the slack. It also shows they may be a leader because they were not afraid to ask when other players who do not understand just stood quietly and hope that they would not get a turn.

So again, speak up. Do not be one of those players who sit back and never say anything and continue to mess up. Communication on the defensive end of the floor is essential in winning. Communicating with your teachers in the classroom is also essential in getting A's instead of F's. Whether on the court or in the classroom, it is important that whatever you are being asked and expected to perform if not clear understanding is stopped before moving on. Think about that time you did not understand how to do a math problem and when you went to do the homework, you still did not understand. Then at test time you received a bad grade. Or that time the coach drew up a play and you really did not know where to go, but you went out there on court and went in the wrong direction and coach sat you down. As of today, do not allow that to happen again.

In closing, remember that your reputation is what people perceive of you. So do not allow teachers and coaches to think that you are not an active participant. They may perceive that as laziness or having a whatever, un-coachable attitude. These players often find themselves in the bleachers watching and not on the floor playing. Do not miss out on the tremendous power of communication. Fully understand that communication is much more then talking. It is also knowing, doing, and listening. Be flexible and adaptive to any situation, be able to talk about any subject manner with substance and knowledge, be able to listen, hear, and incorporate others' ideas, and most importantly communicate, communicate, and always communicate with the complete understanding that communication is more about how it is received than how it is given.

OVERTIME

"HAVE PATIENCE WITH ALL THINGS, BUT CHIEFLY HAVE PATIENCE WITH YOURSELF. DO NOT LOSE COURAGE IN CONSIDERING YOUR OWN IMPERFECTIONS, BUT INSTANTLY SET ABOUT REMEDYING THEM... EVERY DAY, BEGIN THE TASK ANEW."

St. Francis de Sales

CLOSING

"IF YOU'RE TRYING TO ACHIEVE, THERE WILL BE ROADBLOCKS. I'VE HAD THEM; EVERYBODY HAS HAD THEM. BUT OBSTACLES DON'T HAVE TO STOP YOU. IF YOU RUN INTO A WALL, DON'T TURN AROUND AND GIVE UP. FIGURE OUT HOW TO CLIMB IT, GO THROUGH IT, OR WORK AROUND IT. "

Michael Jordan

At the time, I did not recognize or maybe even care that my decision in high school was going to be a life changing one. Looking back on the decision to follow the in-crowd may have caused me a chance to be not the next Pele, but instead the first Jimmie L. Lucas. However, I did not allow one bad decision to stop me. I still ended up in college playing soccer as well as professional basketball in Germany and Okinawa, and although I may have missed out on the opportunity to represent my country in a World Cup, I believe that I am now doing exactly what I was meant to do all along.

My experiences in life have given me the opportunity to give something back to those who might need a little guidance. I can tell you to never give up on your dream and that it is never too late to start again or to finish the task. It is up to you to go out and do it at all costs. The most important and hardest thing is taking that first step. Each step after that becomes easier and easier. I will not lie to you and say things will be smoother if you simply take my advice, because that will be false. What I will tell you is that if you take my advice, you will place yourself in a position to achieve everything you want in life. All I can do is get you to the top of the hill, but it will be up to you whether you roll back down or push higher. Making it to the top cannot be where you decide to stop. Kobe and LeBron were at the top when their names were called in the first round of the NBA draft. However, that is not where they stopped. Instead, they kept fighting, kept pushing, kept going, to where they now sit at the top of that mountain as two of the greatest to ever put on a pair of basketball shoes.

Life is full of unexpected things that will occur during the course of your journey to achieving success. You will face many failures, but Michael Jordan put it best when he said, "I have failed over and over again, and that is why I succeed." What is meant by this is that with each failure comes a lesson, and with each lesson comes growth and ultimately a new success. So, when road blocks are placed in front you, remember that what is on the other side is a lot better to face than what you left behind.

In closing remember this: good coaches will look for the 7 C's when analyzing individual players. You will get pushed far beyond your comfort zone; however, you now have the **CAPABILITY** to stay the course. Your **CONFIDENCE** is vital to your success and performance. You must **CONSISTENTLY** do things the right way all the time, regardless of outside negative influences, as you completely become **COMMITTED** to your dreams and goals. Be a person of high **CHARACTER**, because that is what counts more then your reputation. The reality here is that you are aware of how much it will **COST** to be a successful player and a person that is able to **COMMUNICATE** effectively with everyone and anyone.

The ball is in your hands, so do not turn it over…

POST GAME COOL DOWN

CHAMPIONS AREN'T MADE IN THE GYMS. CHAMPIONS ARE MADE FROM SOMETHING THEY HAVE DEEP INSIDE THEM—A DESIRE, A DREAM, A VISION.

Muhammad Ali

ACKNOWLEDGEMENT

First to the Creator of all things. Thank you for blessing me with the words throughout these pages. You understand me in knowing that I write books not for fame or fortune but rather to move generations in positive directions. To inspire those who are looking for encouragement and to be a light for those walking in darkness. Thank you for granting me with your grace and mercy and providing my journey with covering and anointing.

To my mother, that taught me as well as showed me what being a servant of God truly is. That there is always somebody who has it worse than I do and therefore I should always look for opportunities to serve selflessly.

Those special people in my life, who have always been there for me, regardless of or disagreements and misunderstandings. Your continued and unwavering support continues to give me the inspiration to do what I truly love. Thank you for all your support.

To everyone who have read this book, I thank you. My prayer is that within these pages, there was something that gave you hope and an avenue towards turning all your dreams into a reality. Even if it is not basketball, apply these 7 C's throughout every part of your life, and you will find success for your future. Always remember to believe in self and that hard work always out last talent. Talent will run out and dissolve, but hard work can always be utilized.

FINAL THOUGHTS

"THE JOURNEY IS MORE IMPORTANT THAN THE FINISH LINE. IT'S THE FUN, WORK, AND EXPERIENCES (GOOD AND BAD) ALONG THE WAY THAT ULTIMATELY WILL BE THE MOST VALUABLE TO YOUR PERSONAL GROWTH. IF YOU HAVE PREPARED, WORKED YOUR HARDEST, PLAYED FAIR, AND GIVEN IT YOUR BEST EFFORT ALONG THE WAY, THEN NO MATTER WHAT HAPPENS, YOU CAN BE PROUD AND SATISFIED AT THE END. IF YOU FAIL TO PREPARE, YOU PREPARE TO FAIL."

Coach John Wooden

ABOUT THE AUTHOR:

Jimmie L. Lucas is a Life Coach, behavior specialist, personal trainer, and health coach. Jimmie spent over twenty years in the military and ten years playing professional basketball overseas, where he learned how to mentally prepare as well as learning how physical limitations can be overcome once you understand how to be mentally focus.

www.ingramcontent.com/pod-product-compliance
Lightning Source LLC
LaVergne TN
LVHW012036060526
838201LV00061B/4636